The Roads

by Asa Endo
illustrated by Mircea Catusanu

HOUGHTON MIFFLIN   BOSTON

ISBN 10: 0-618-88684-2
ISBN 13: 978-0-618-88684-5

123456789 STA 16 15 14 13 12 11 10 09 08 07

"I wonder how many potatoes we have,"
said Mom.

"Wow! It could take forever to count all those
potatoes," said Tom. "I've got an idea. Let's put them
in piles of 10."

Read • Think • Write How many potatoes do they have?

2

"We have lots of onions, too," said Tom.

"We sure do," said Mom. "Let's count them."

"We could put them in lines," said Tom.

Read • Think • Write How many onions do they have?

3

"People always like our lettuce," said Mom.

"I put our lettuce in rows like this. We can count by tens and then add ones."

Read•Think•Write How many heads of lettuce do they have?

4

"These tomatoes look so juicy, don't they Mom?" asked Tom. "I think people are going to buy them right away. Let's use tens to add them."

Read•Think•Write How many tomatoes do Tom and his mother have?

"Corn is my favorite vegetable," said Tom. "I hope we don't sell all of it!"

His mom laughed. "We'll see. There's an easy way to count the ears of corn."

Read • Think • Write How many ears of corn do Mom and Tom have?

"It's only noon and we have already sold a lot of vegetables," said Mom. "We make a good team." We sure do," said Tom.

Let Us Count Lettuce

Show

Look at page 4. Draw a picture to show how many heads of lettuce you see.

Share

Draw Conclusions Talk about how many tens and how many ones you see on page 4. Tell if it is easier to count each vegetable by ones or by tens.

Write

Write about the rows of vegetables you see on page 4. Write how many heads of lettuce there are.